Shadows of Finds: One Day on Wyre in Orkney

Jeanne Bouza Rose

Tracing around Neolithic small finds, positioned with the small finds unearthed in 2012.

Photos and poetry put into place 2023.

PUBISHED by Tidal Waters Press

Paperback edition ISBN 978-1-959318-25-5

https://tidalwaterspress.com

I dedicate this book to Antonia Thomas who has helped feed my interest in Neolithic marks/art in Orkney. And to Dan Lee who also allowed me to be part of their dig on Wyre. April 21, 2023

And to my sister, who is the writer and publisher in my life! xx

INTRODUCTION

In 2010, I arrived from the USA for a long stay on Orkney and by the spring of 2012, I was well immersed in Orkney's active archaeological activities. Particularly smitten by the Neolithic, I arrived in 2010 already following the work of archaeologist, Antonia Thomas. She was researching the "art" of the Neolithic and I was a fan. I volunteered at the Ness of Brodgar excavation starting in 2011.

I found Antonia to be a neighbour of mine in Stromness. She was the site director of an ongoing dig on the island of Wyre at the Brae o' Habreck, discovered in 2006, after a fieldwalking exercise. Both she and Dan Lee helped research this complex and have established it as a site for one of the largest assemblages of Neolithic cereal in Scotland.

Early in 2011, offered to help Antonia and Dan for one day on one of Scotland's tiniest islands, Wyre. Without much hands-on archaeological experience, they set me up very graciously, to clean the small finds. You might imagine their continued joy at find minute bits of cereal on the base floor of the dig. So many bits of grain and cereal were found. Not long after this day, they published a paper in <u>ANTIQUITY</u>, October, 2012 which details the types of grain and cereals found in a charred building and theorizes about the structure's use. They were very excited about these tiny finds the day I joined them.

By the time I got on site, many worked tools had also been found. These immediately caught my attention. I began to fall in love with the beauty of Neolithic worked stone objects as I was carefully cleaning them. I felt like I was the guardian of their history as they were washed and laid to dry in the sun.

The sun was strong and the grass very green. I marveled as I caressed these small stone beauties that were both hard and smooth. I had not known what to expect and had the simplest of art materials with me. I wondered how I could best use a felt-tip marker and a sketchpad in the bright sun. I was compelled to transfer whatever I was feeling in my hands into some kind of visual image, not just by using a camera. It was clear that I was caught up with stone objects, and not the tiny grains that were making Antonia and Dan so excited. I could do something artistic with stones.

With the bright sun casting strong shadows, I played with placing the worked stone on the white paper and noticed the interplay of the stone and its shadow. I started to trace the actual stones, very carefully so as to not mark their surface. I turned them over and around and marked their shadows onto the blinding white paper. Each stone had a unique quality and form as I danced them around the paper.

What you will see are my photographs from that day, of the worked stones' dance in sun and shadow with marker on paper. I wasn't always the best photographer, but I hope, the idea still comes through.

The stone "choreography" on one day in 2012, was thus recorded.

I found myself musing over words, images, sentences and jotted some of these thoughts on the backs of the shadow drawings . I have worked these up a bit and hope these create a deeper understanding of this day's work. Perhaps, it is poetry. Perhaps it just one day, one moment.

The site has been covered over and research and the small finds are all that remain. These pages are a few of the small finds' shadow dances. Whatever you may think, none of this will never be possible again. 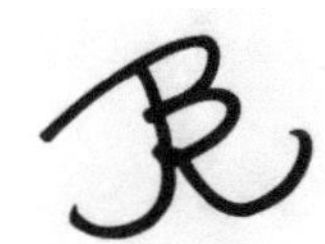

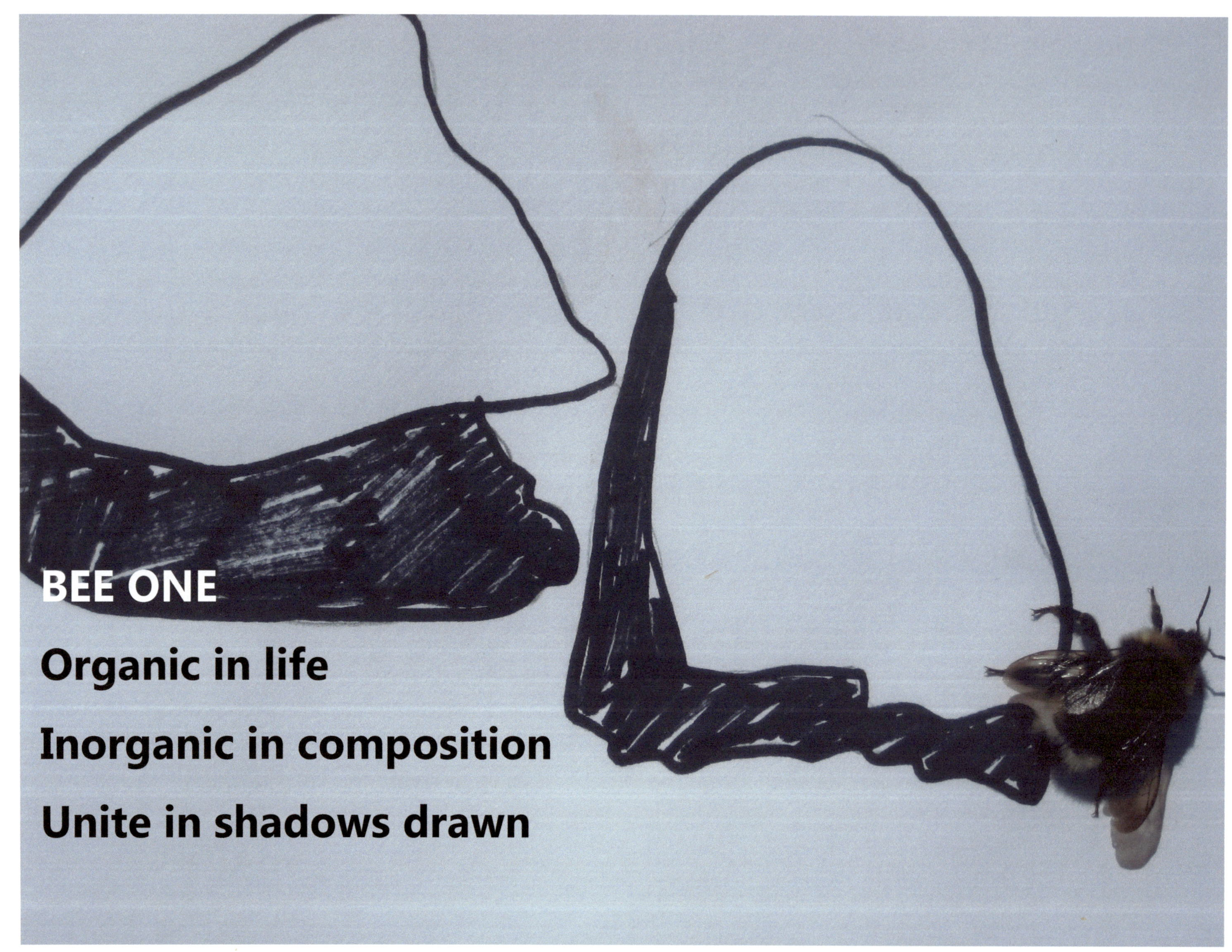

BEE ONE

Organic in life

Inorganic in composition

Unite in shadows drawn

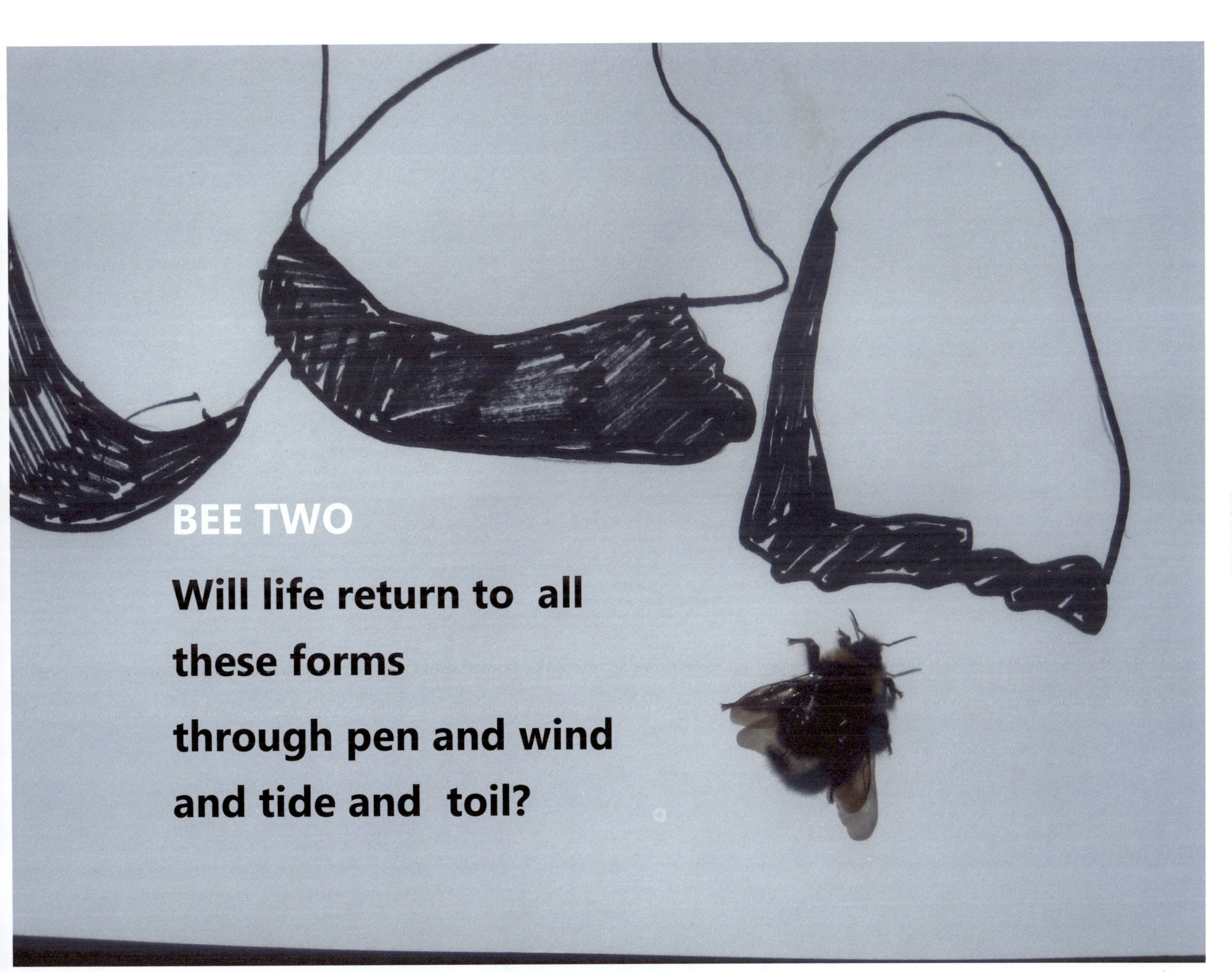

BEE TWO

Will life return to all
these forms
through pen and wind
and tide and toil?

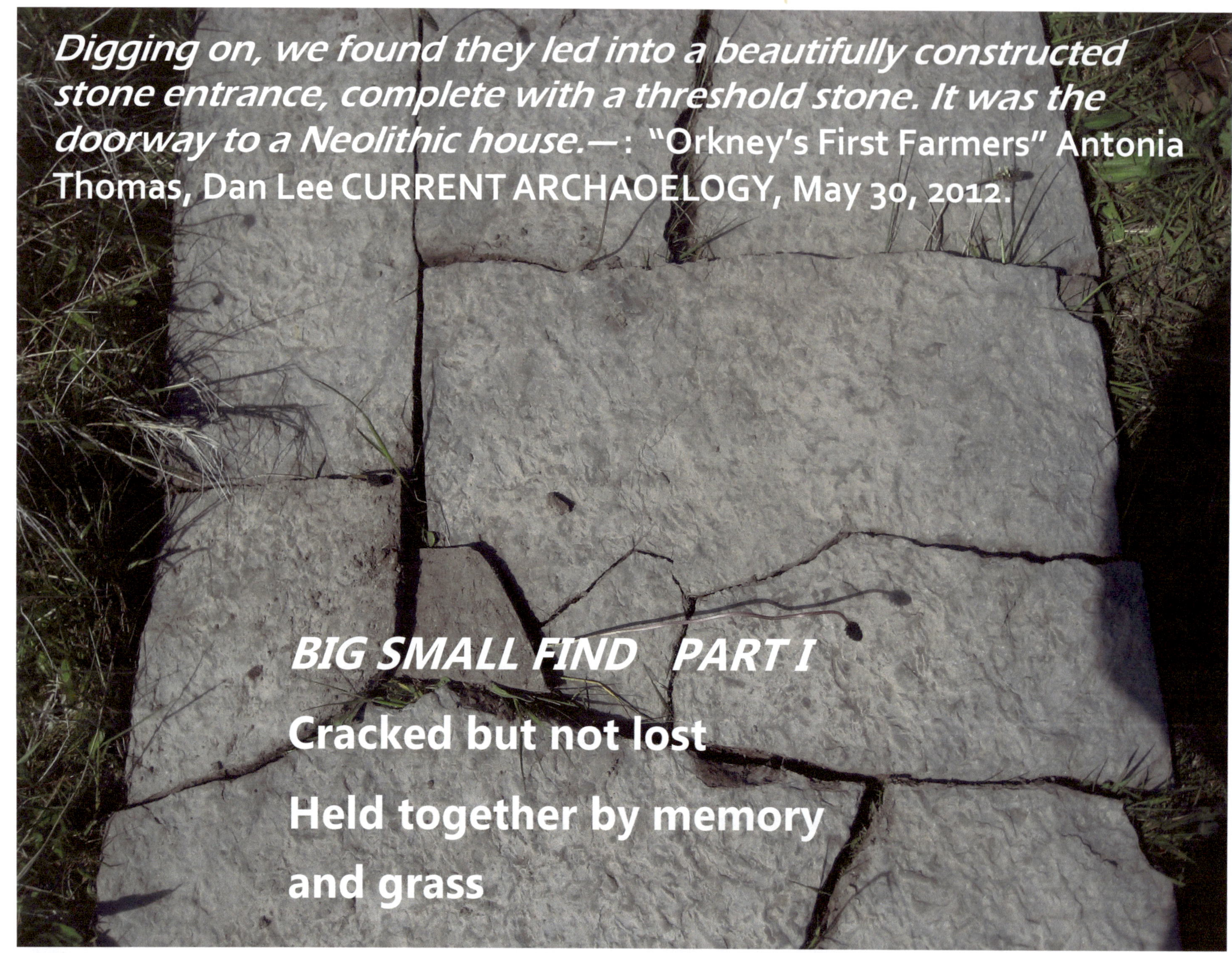
Digging on, we found they led into a beautifully constructed stone entrance, complete with a threshold stone. It was the doorway to a Neolithic house.—: "Orkney's First Farmers" Antonia Thomas, Dan Lee CURRENT ARCHAOELOGY, May 30, 2012.

BIG SMALL FIND   PART I

Cracked but not lost

Held together by memory

and grass

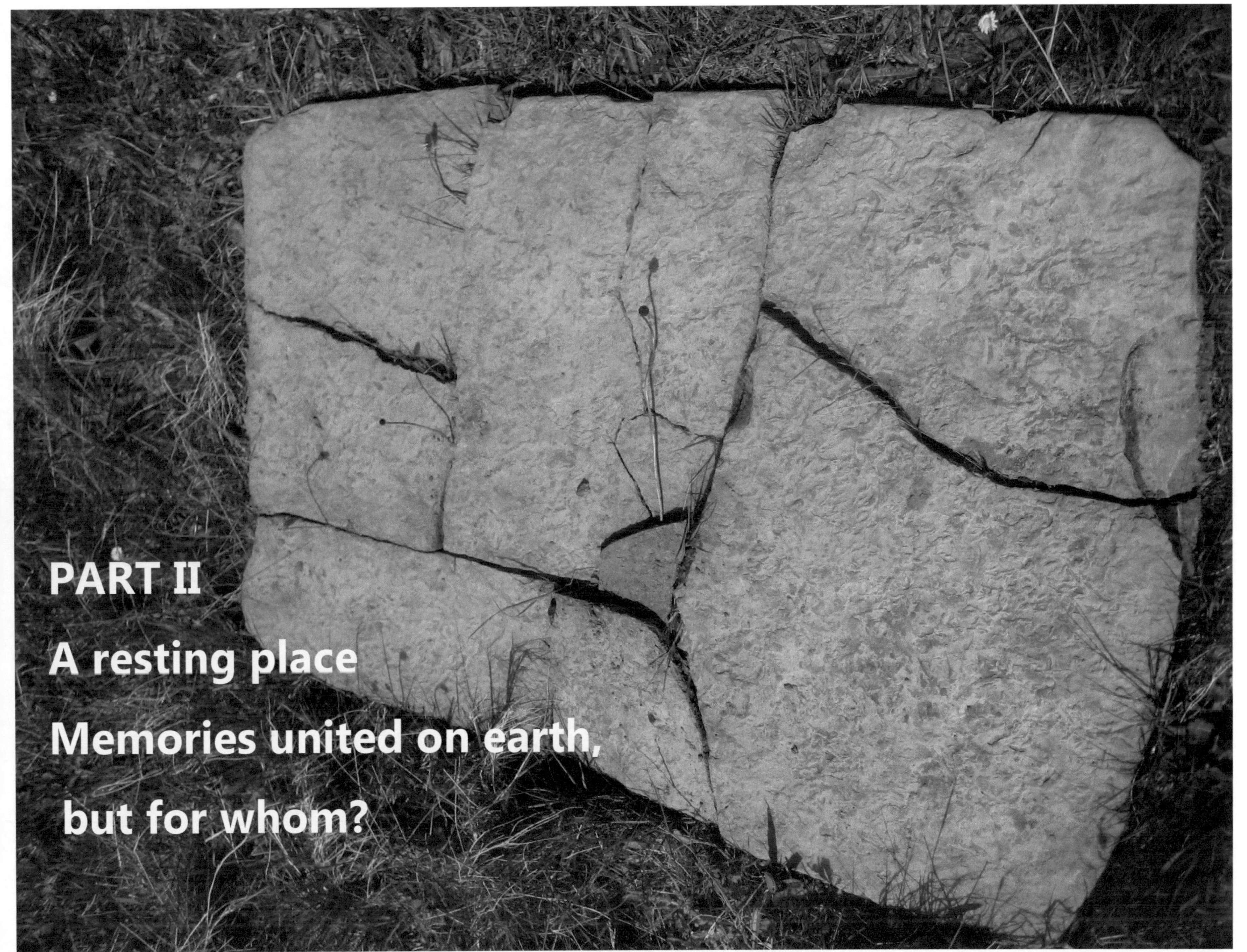
PART II
A resting place
Memories united on earth,
but for whom?

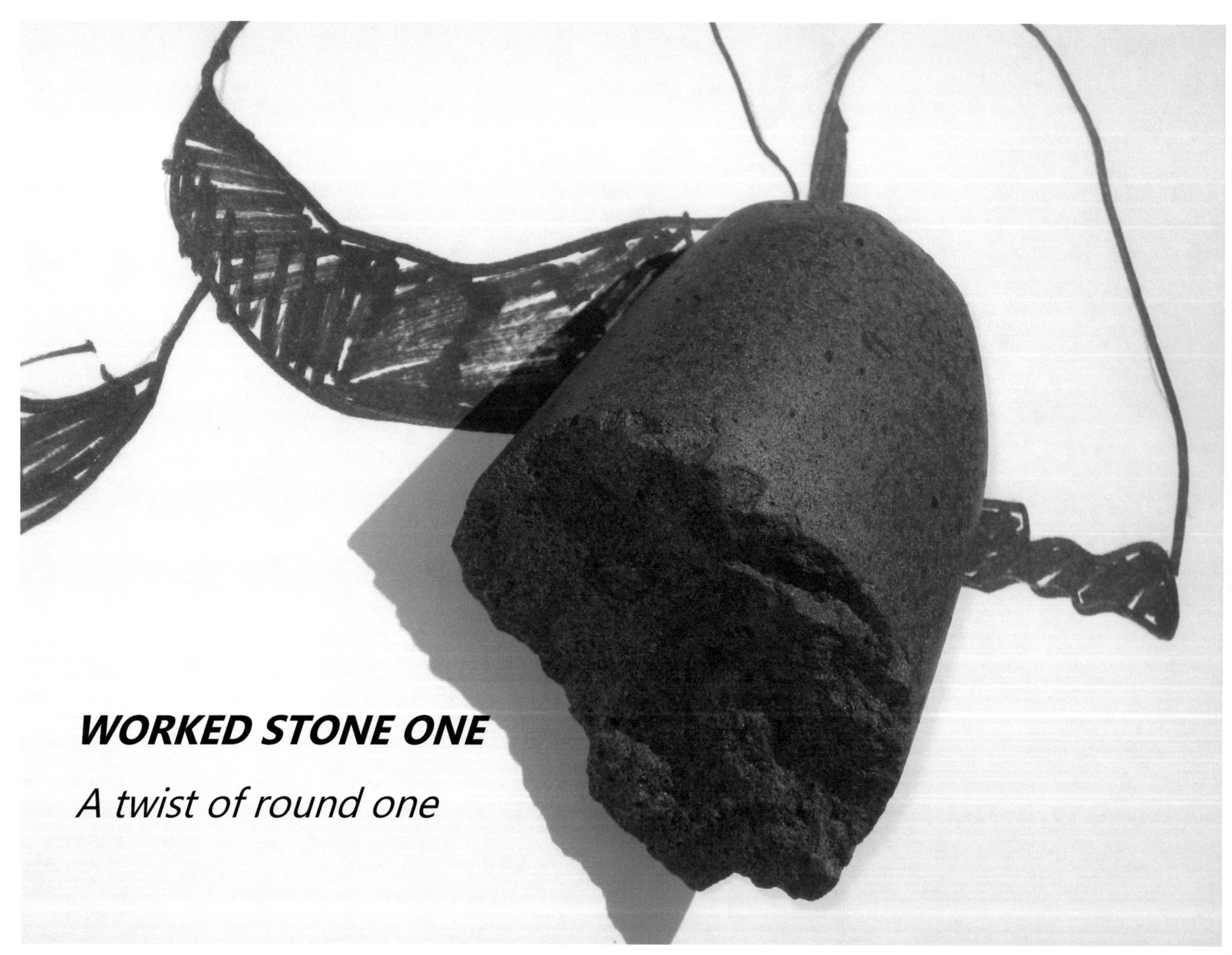

WORKED STONE ONE

A twist of round one

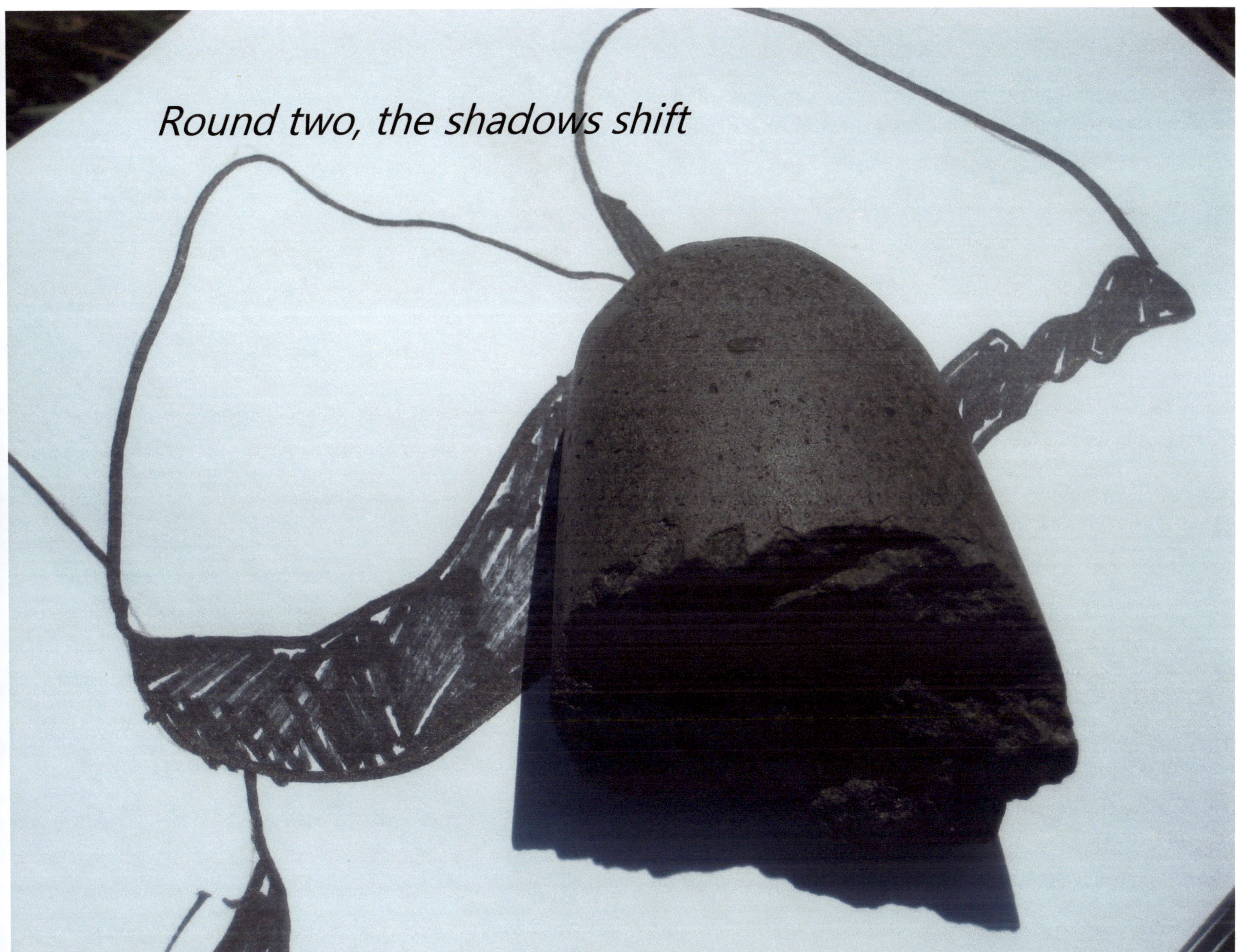

Round two, the shadows shift

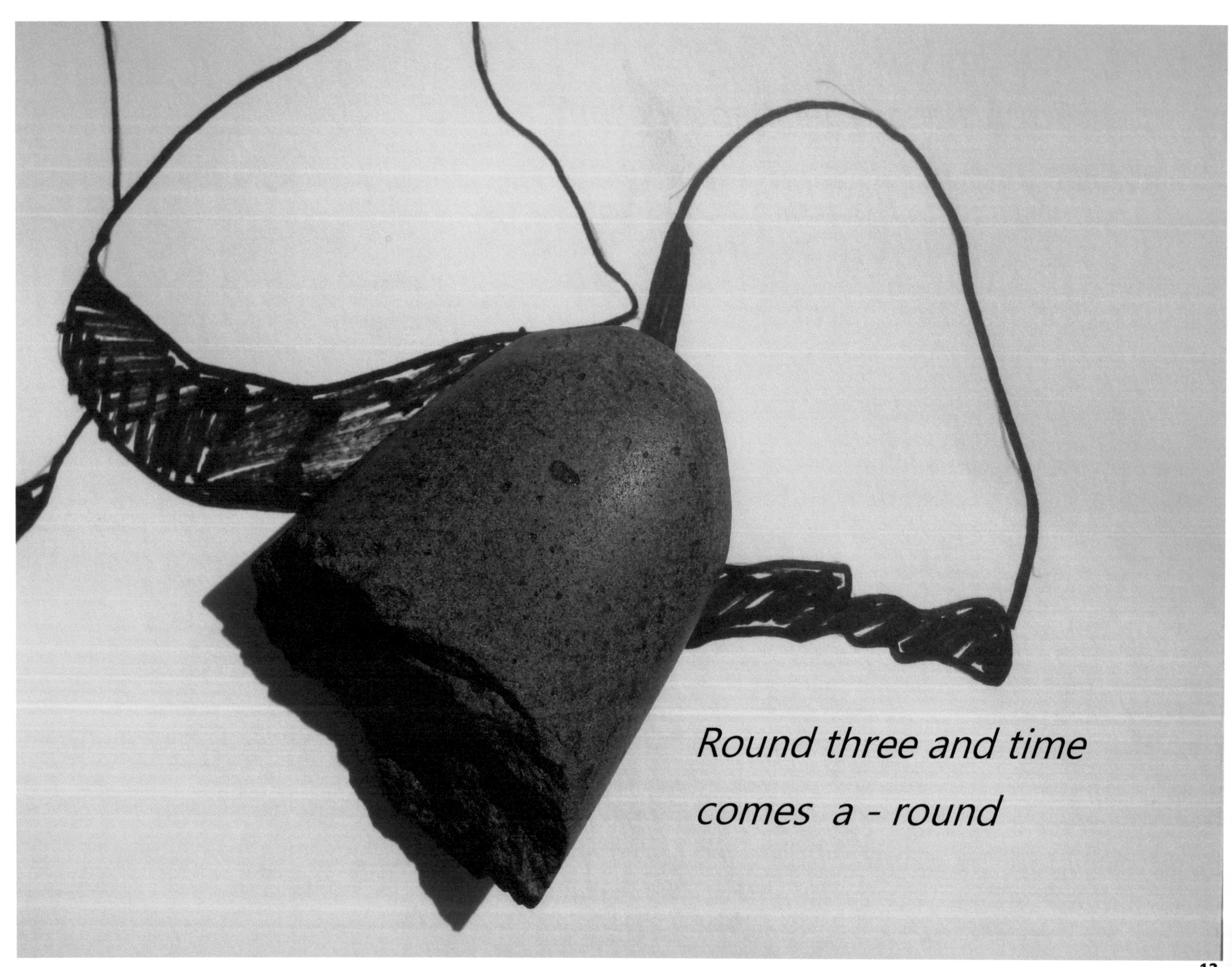

Round three and time

comes a - round

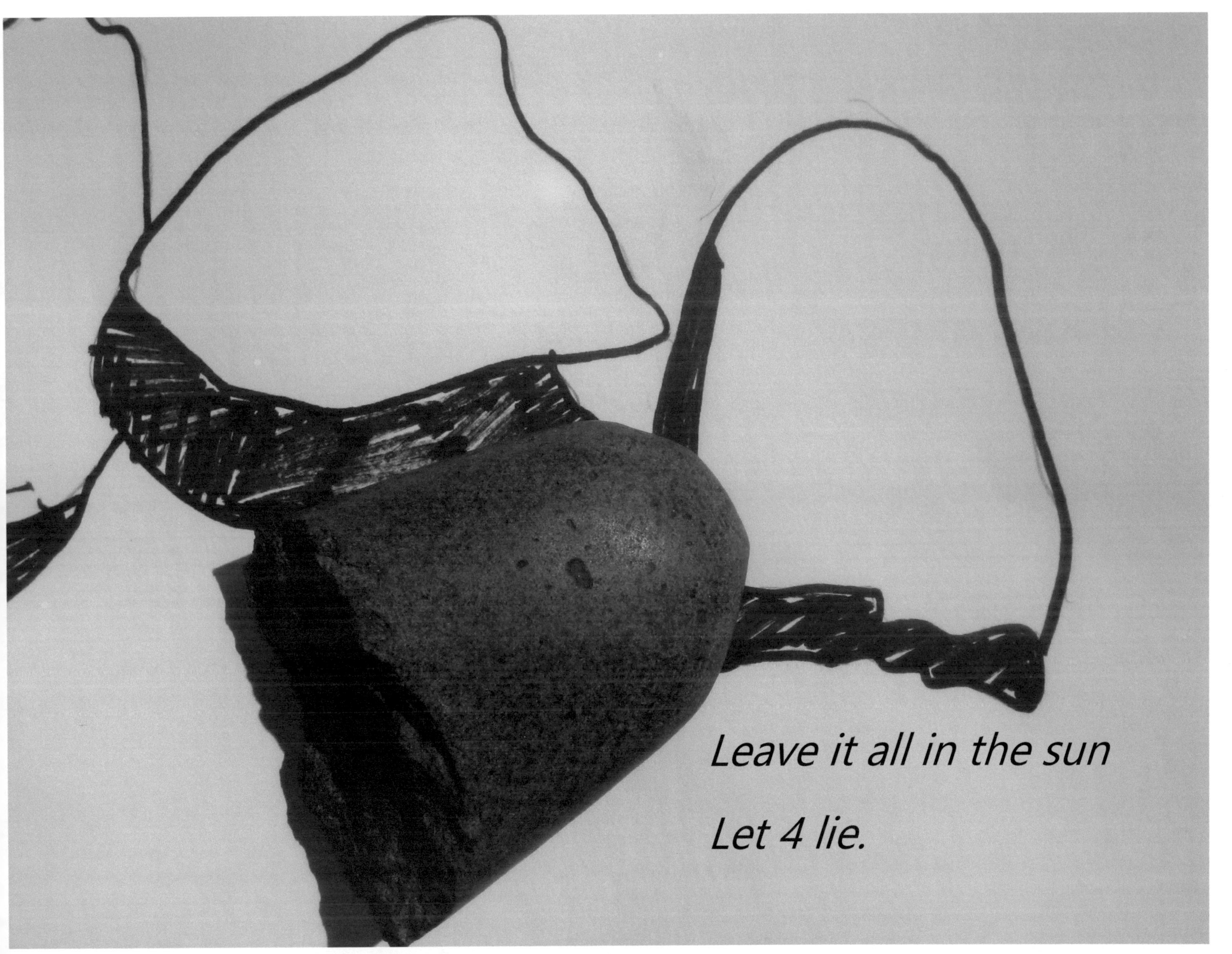

Leave it all in the sun
Let 4 lie.

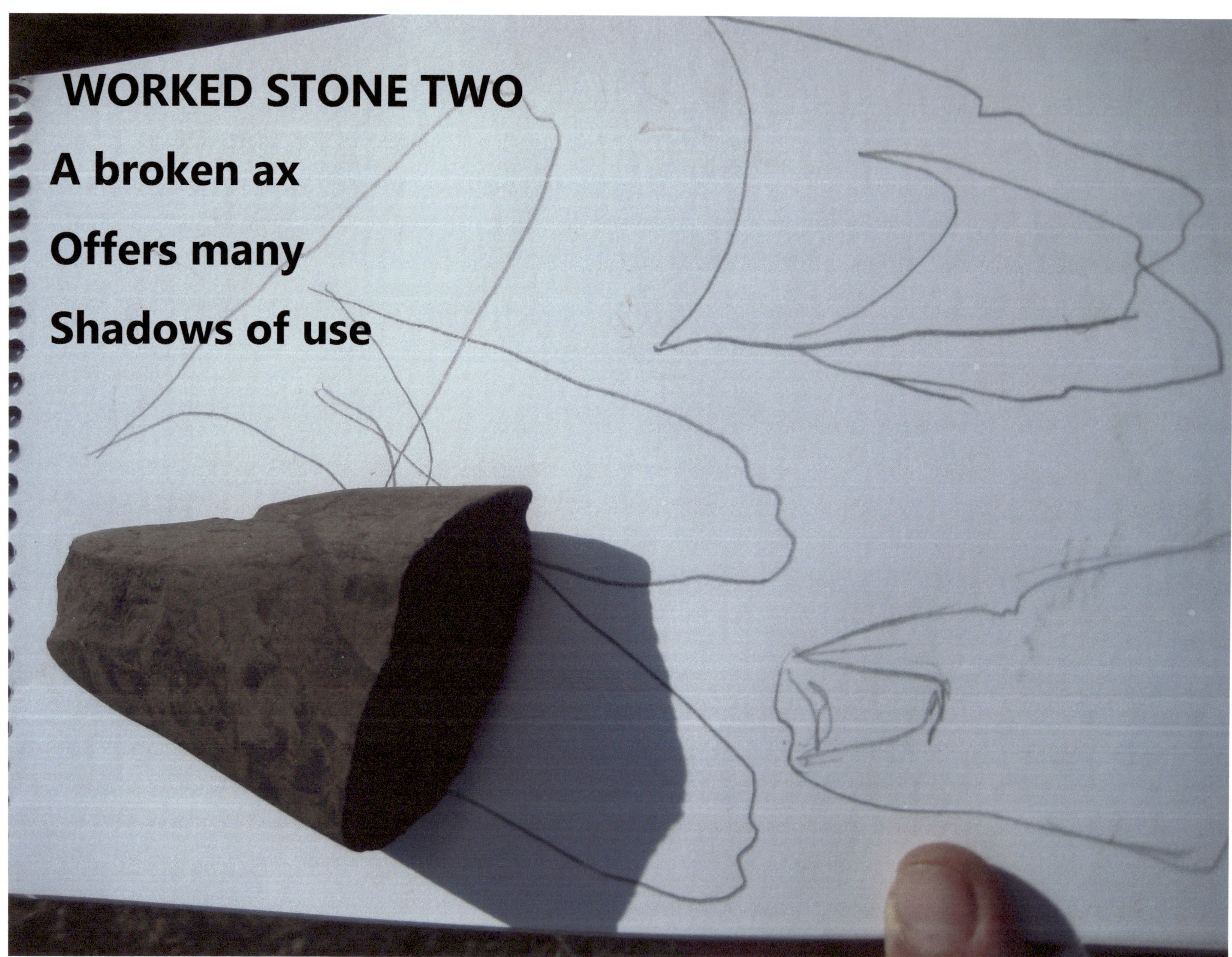

WORKED STONE TWO

A broken ax

Offers many

Shadows of use

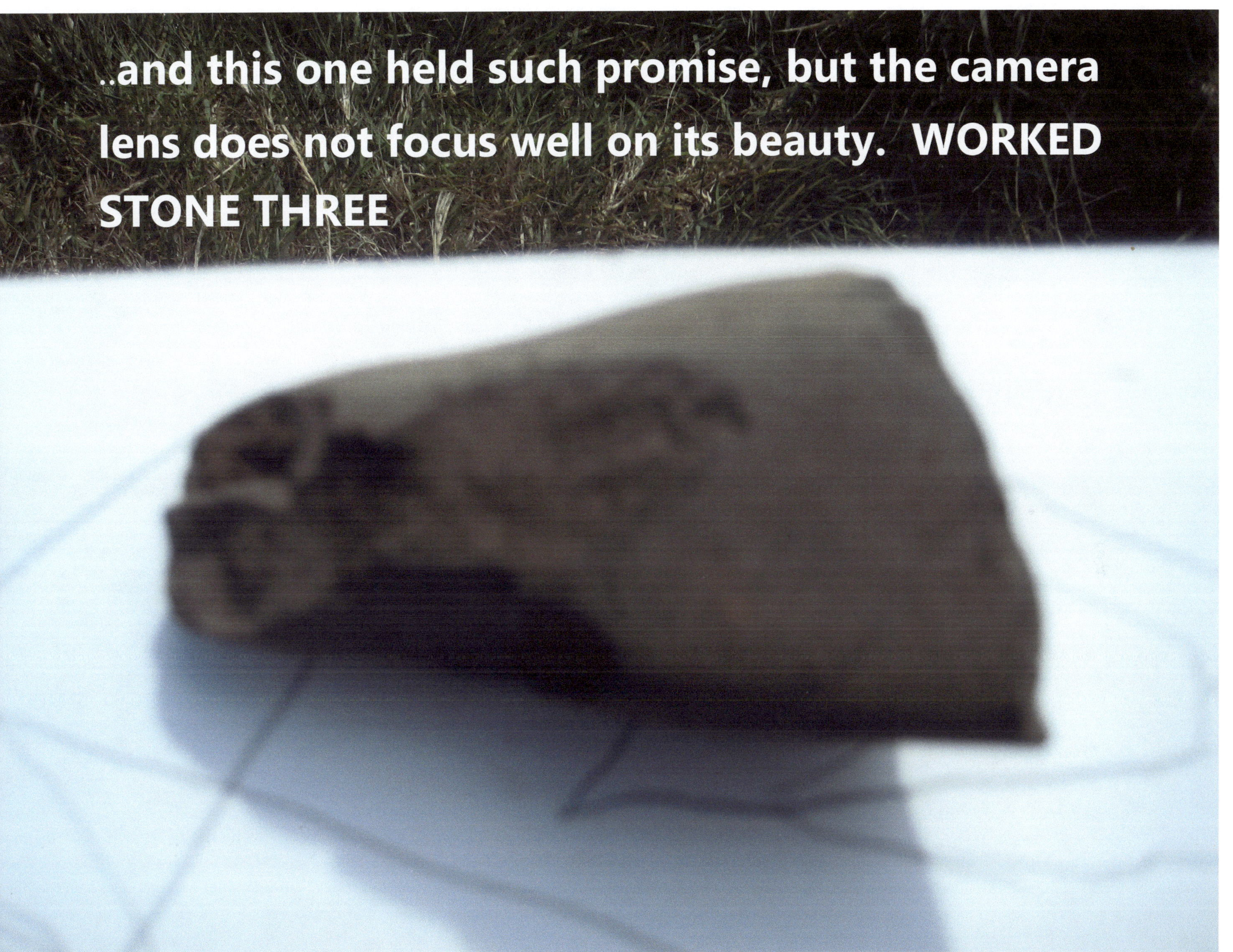
..and this one held such promise, but the camera lens does not focus well on its beauty. WORKED STONE THREE

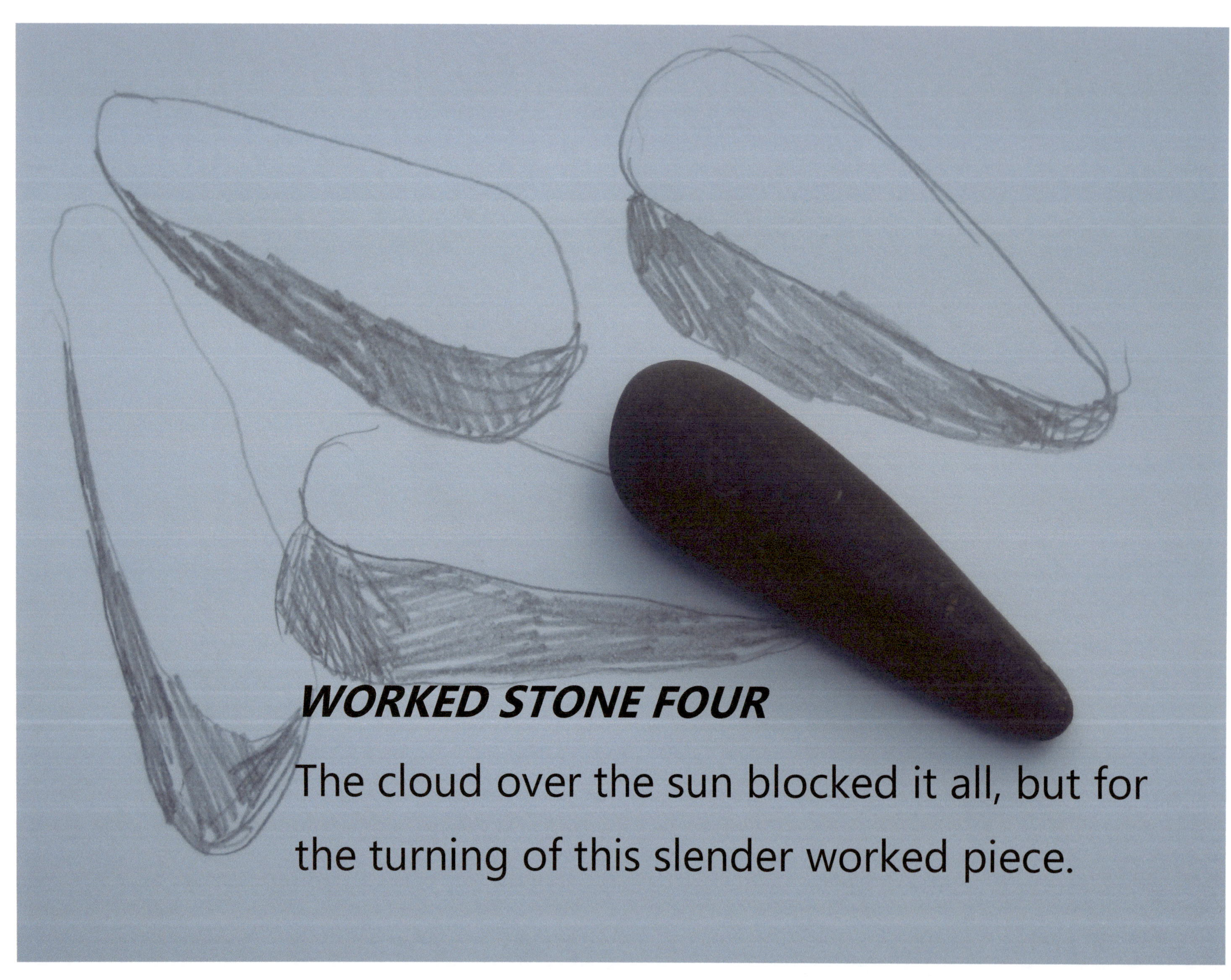

WORKED STONE FOUR

The cloud over the sun blocked it all, but for
the turning of this slender worked piece.

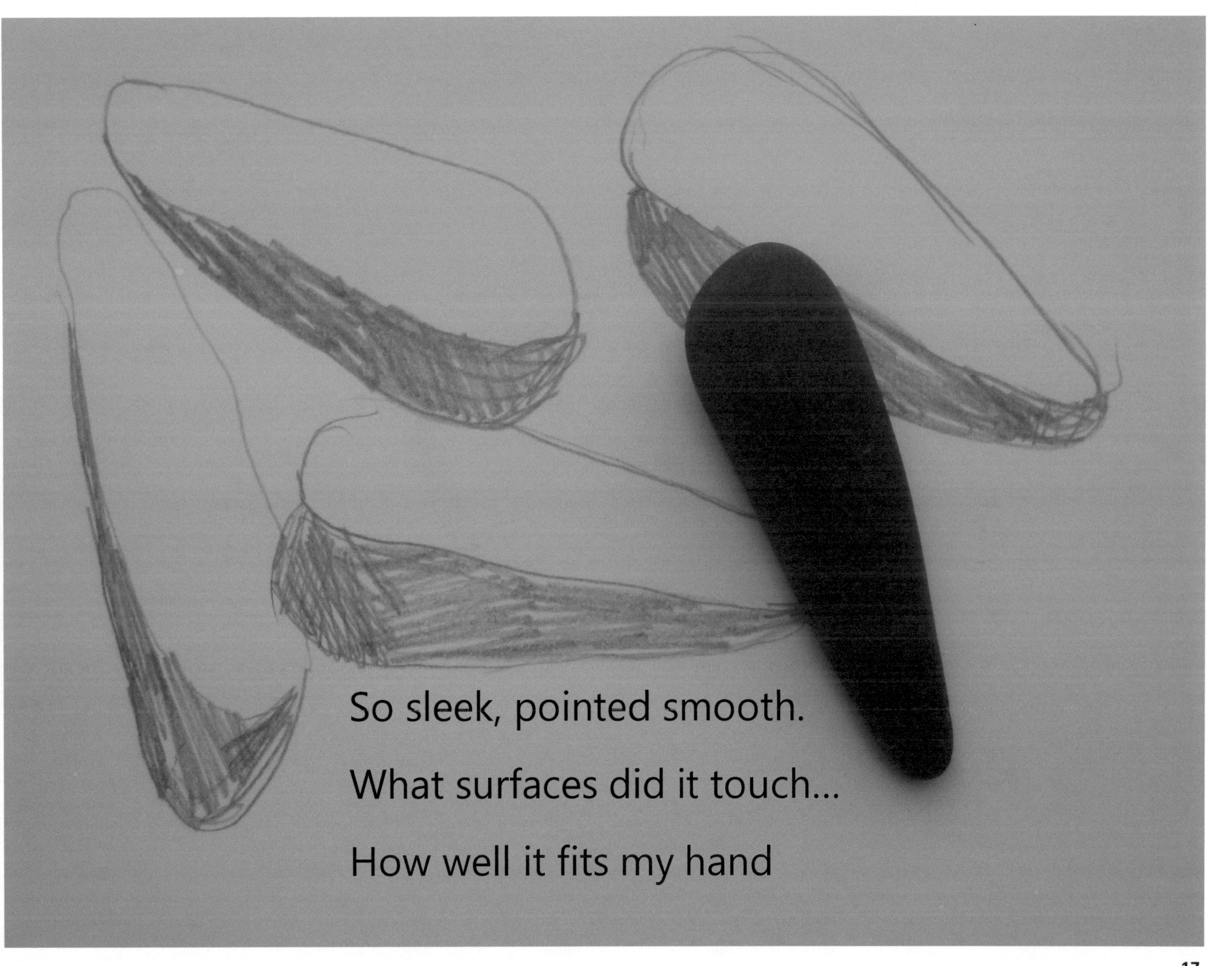
So sleek, pointed smooth.

What surfaces did it touch...

How well it fits my hand

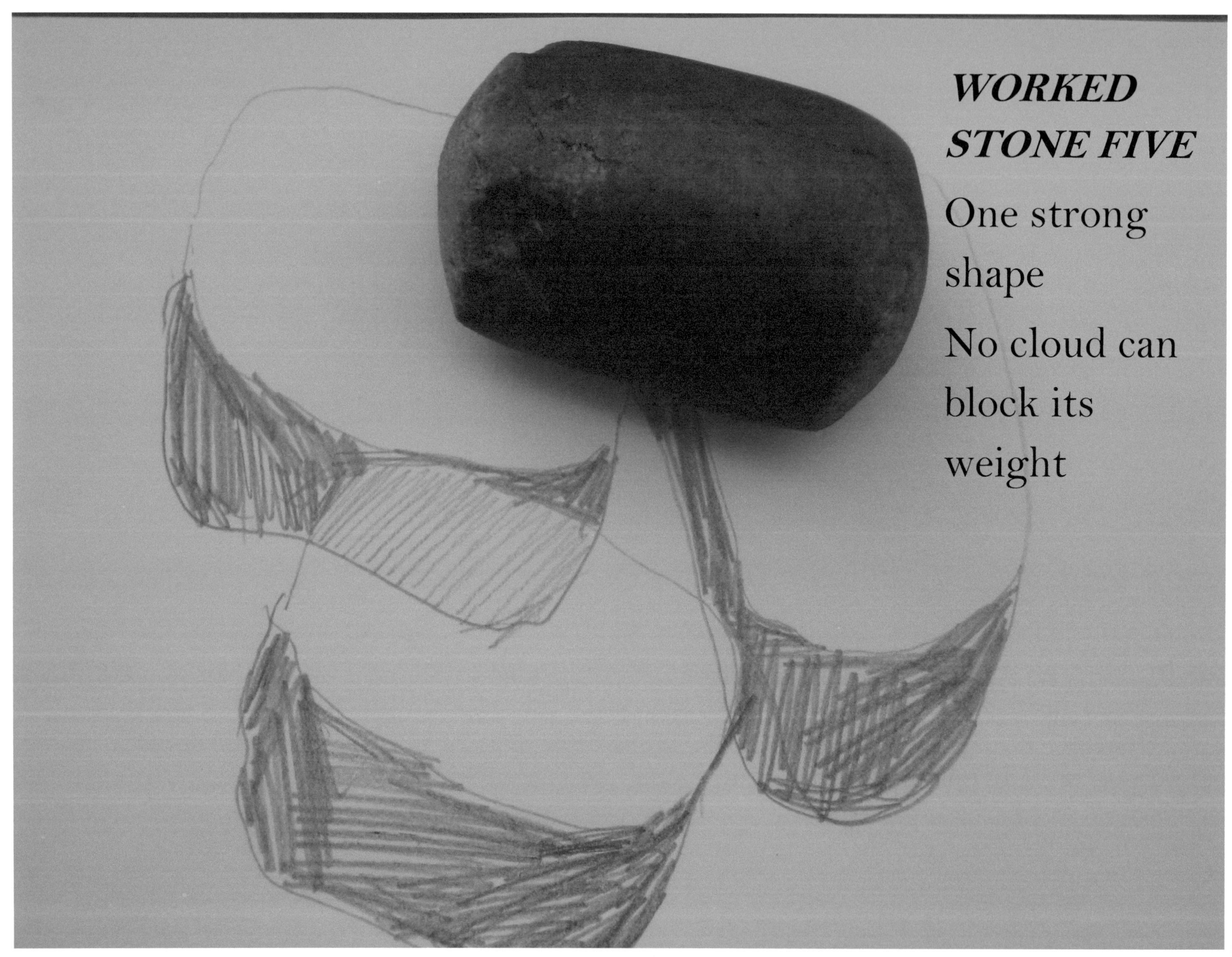

WORKED
STONE FIVE
One strong
shape
No cloud can
block its
weight

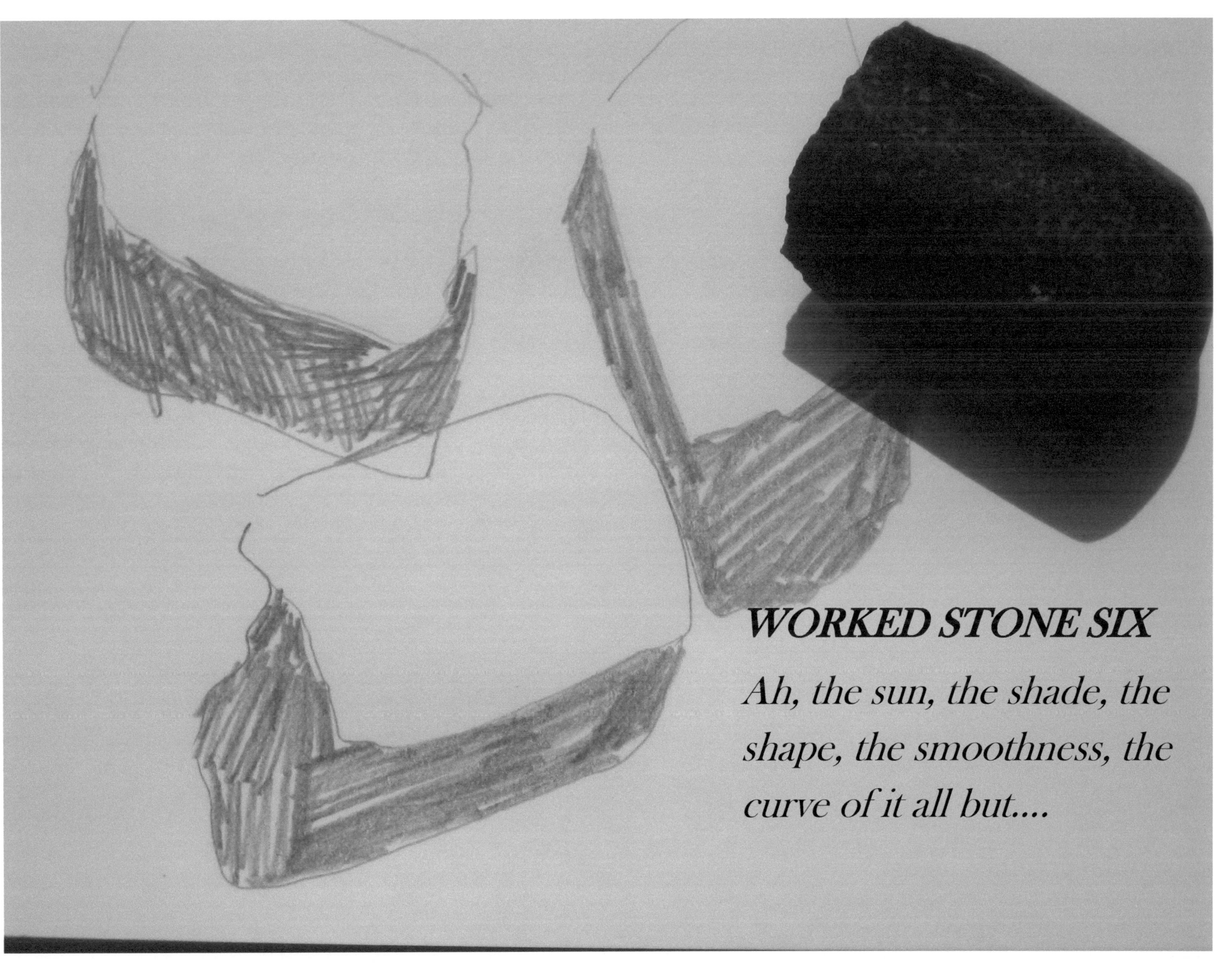
WORKED STONE SIX

Ah, the sun, the shade, the
shape, the smoothness, the
curve of it all but....

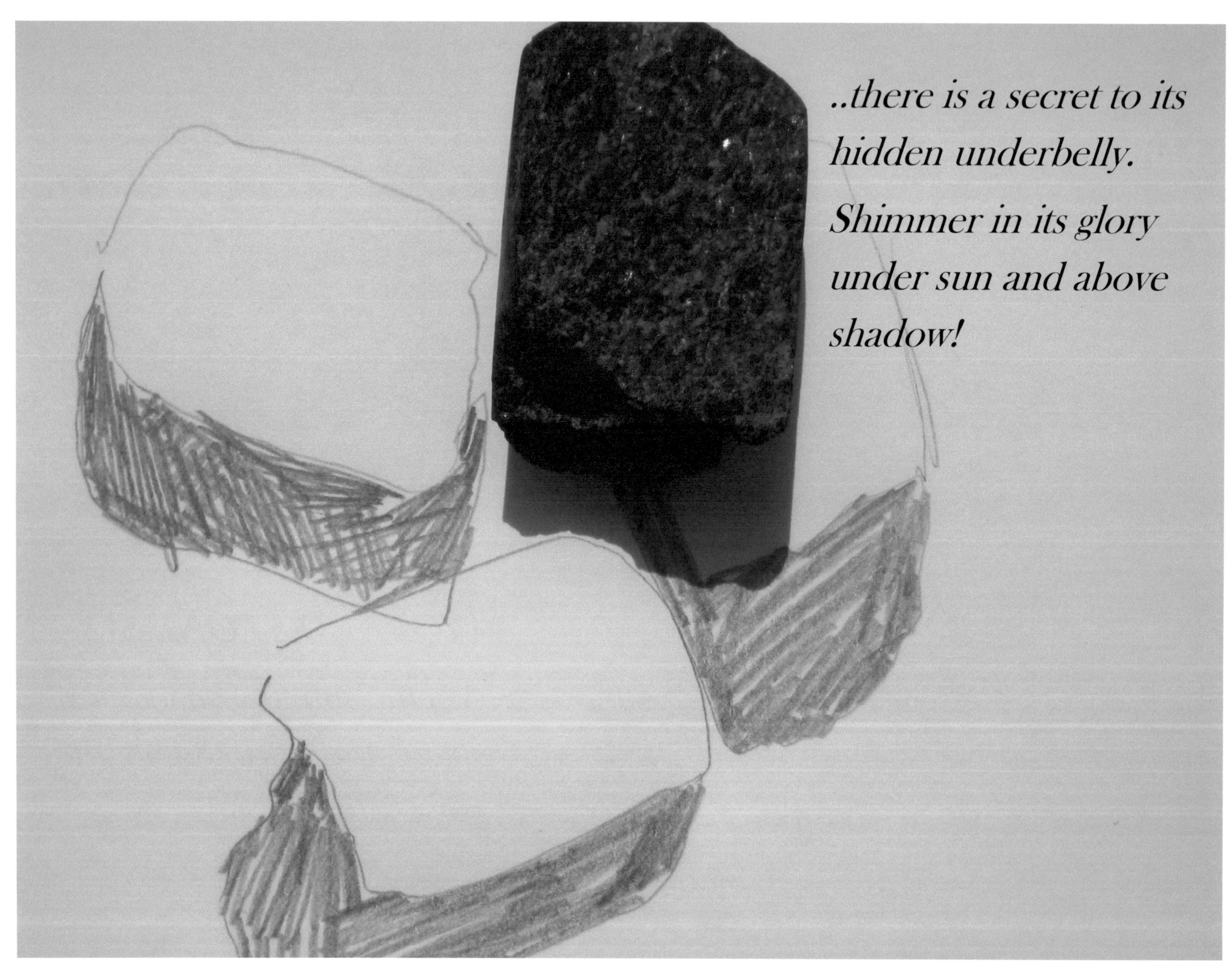

..there is a secret to its hidden underbelly.
Shimmer in its glory under sun and above shadow!

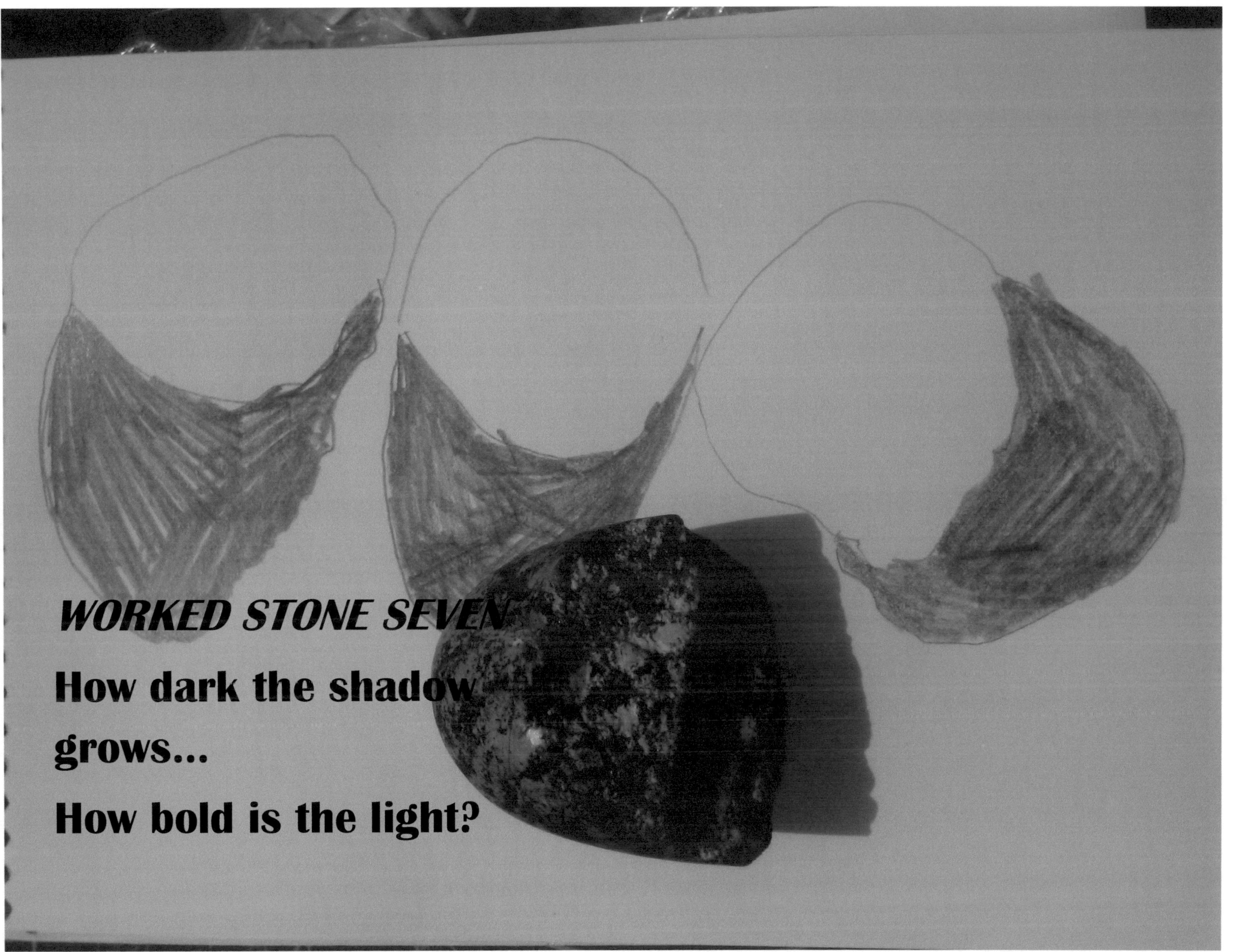

WORKED STONE SEVEN

How dark the shadow
grows...

How bold is the light?

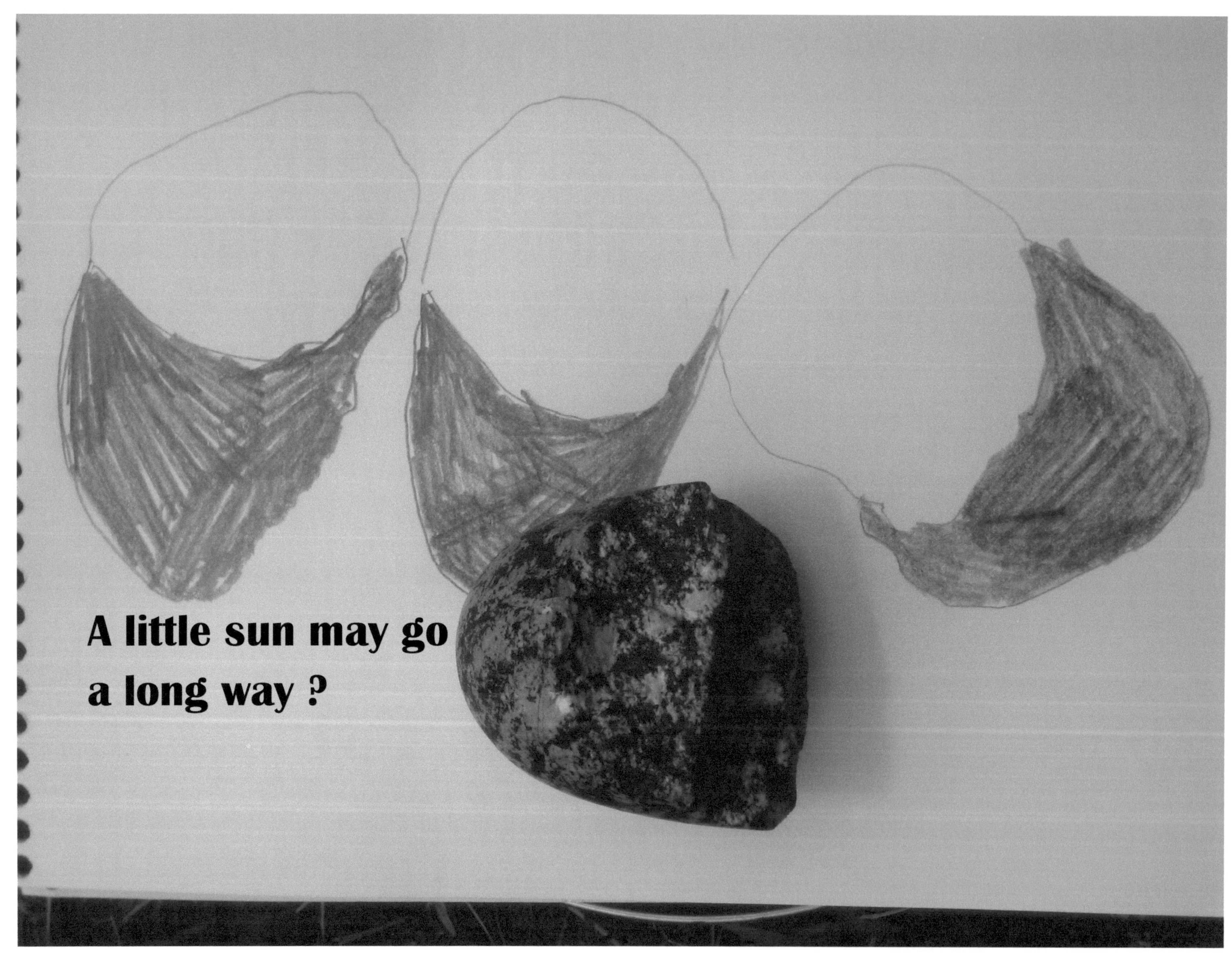
A little sun may go
a long way ?

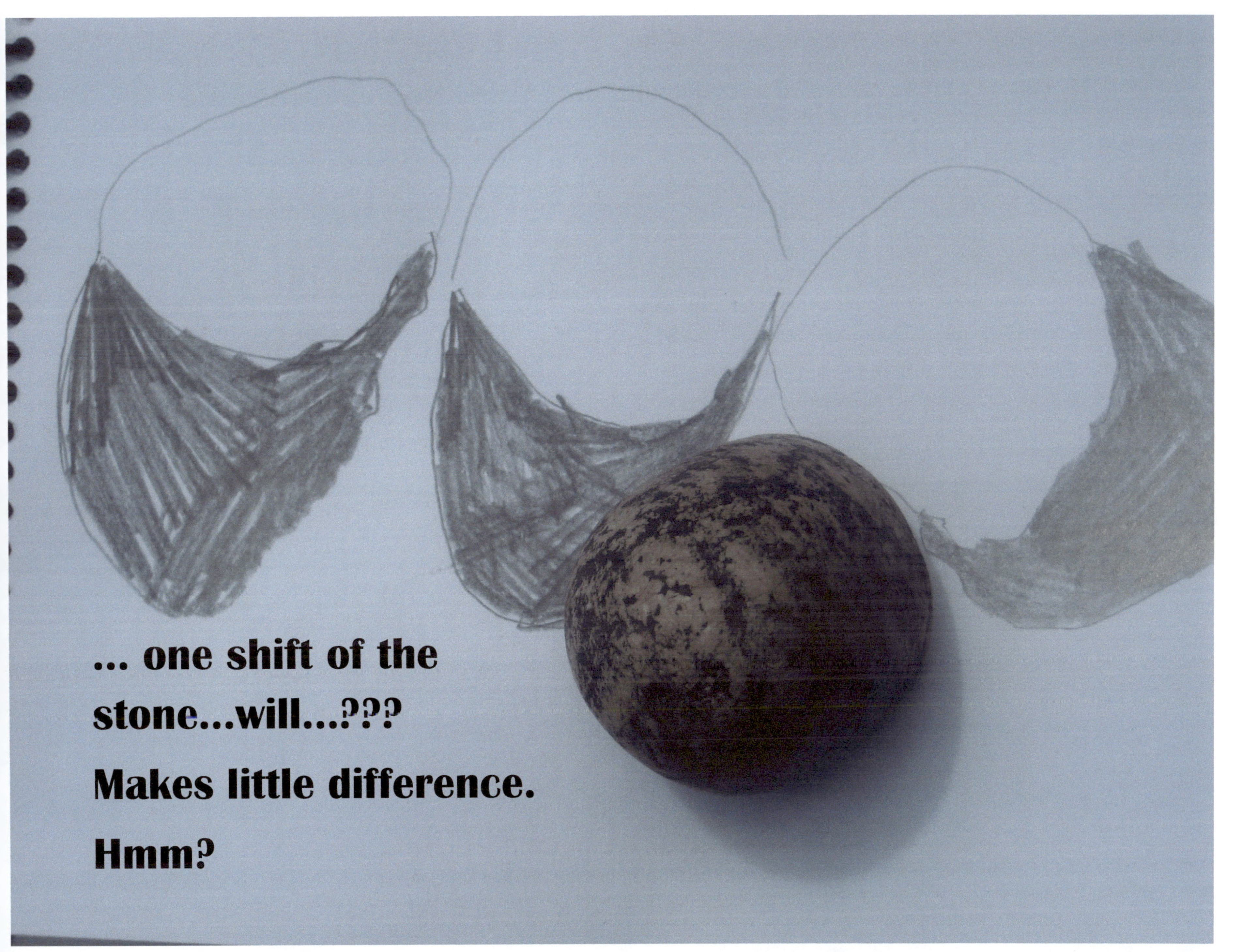
... one shift of the
stone...will...???
Makes little difference.
Hmm?

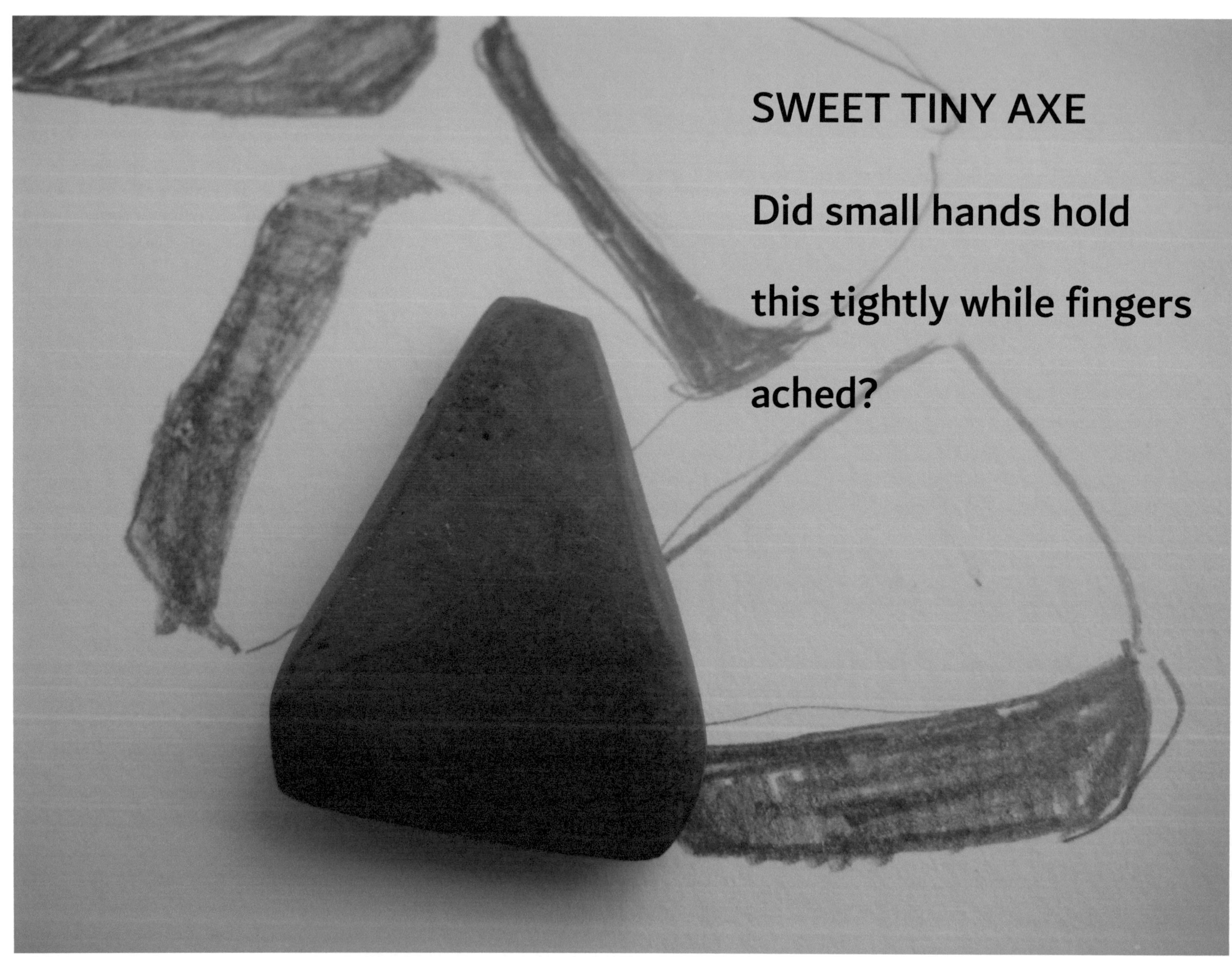
SWEET TINY AXE

Did small hands hold

this tightly while fingers

ached?

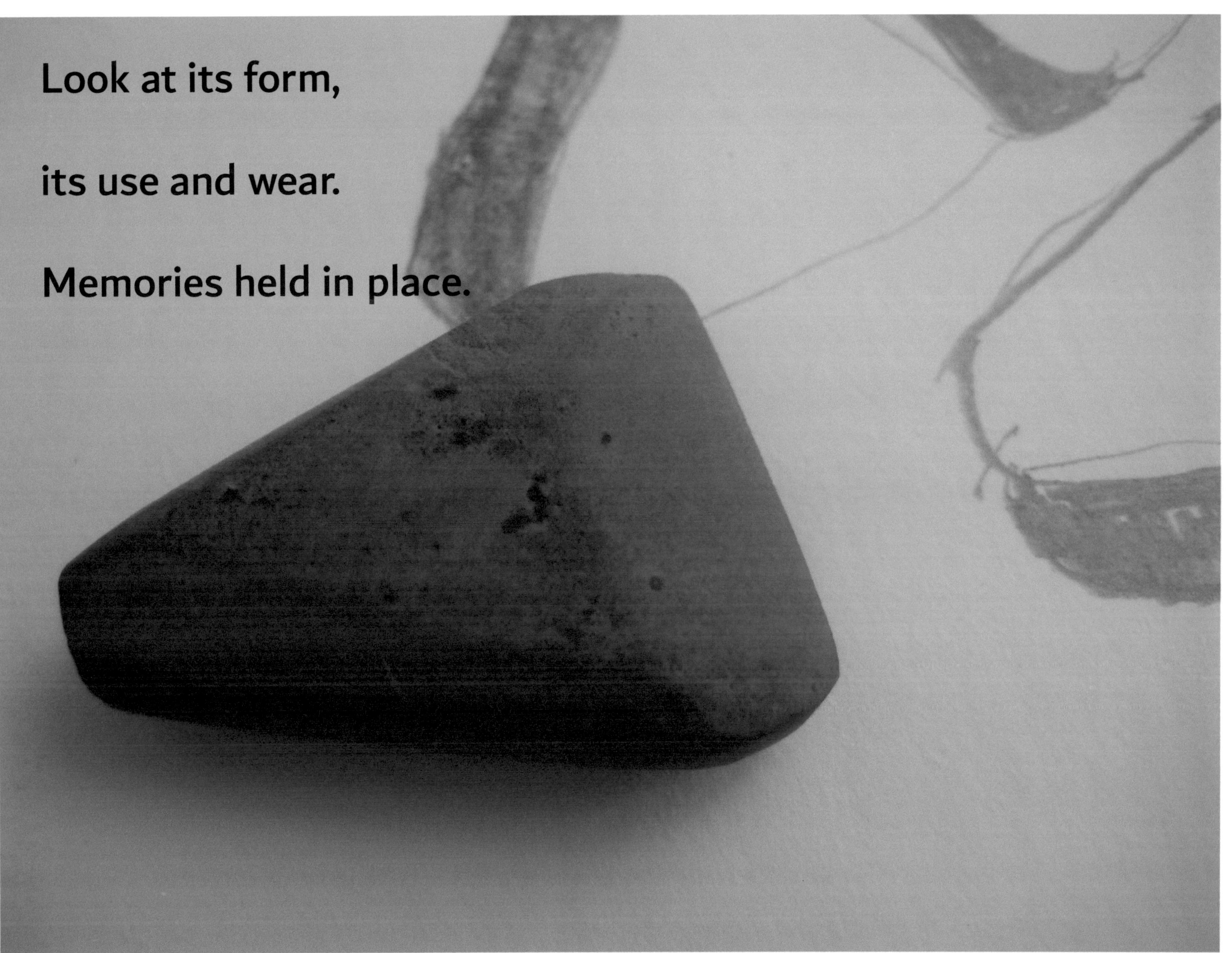
Look at its form,

its use and wear.

Memories held in place.

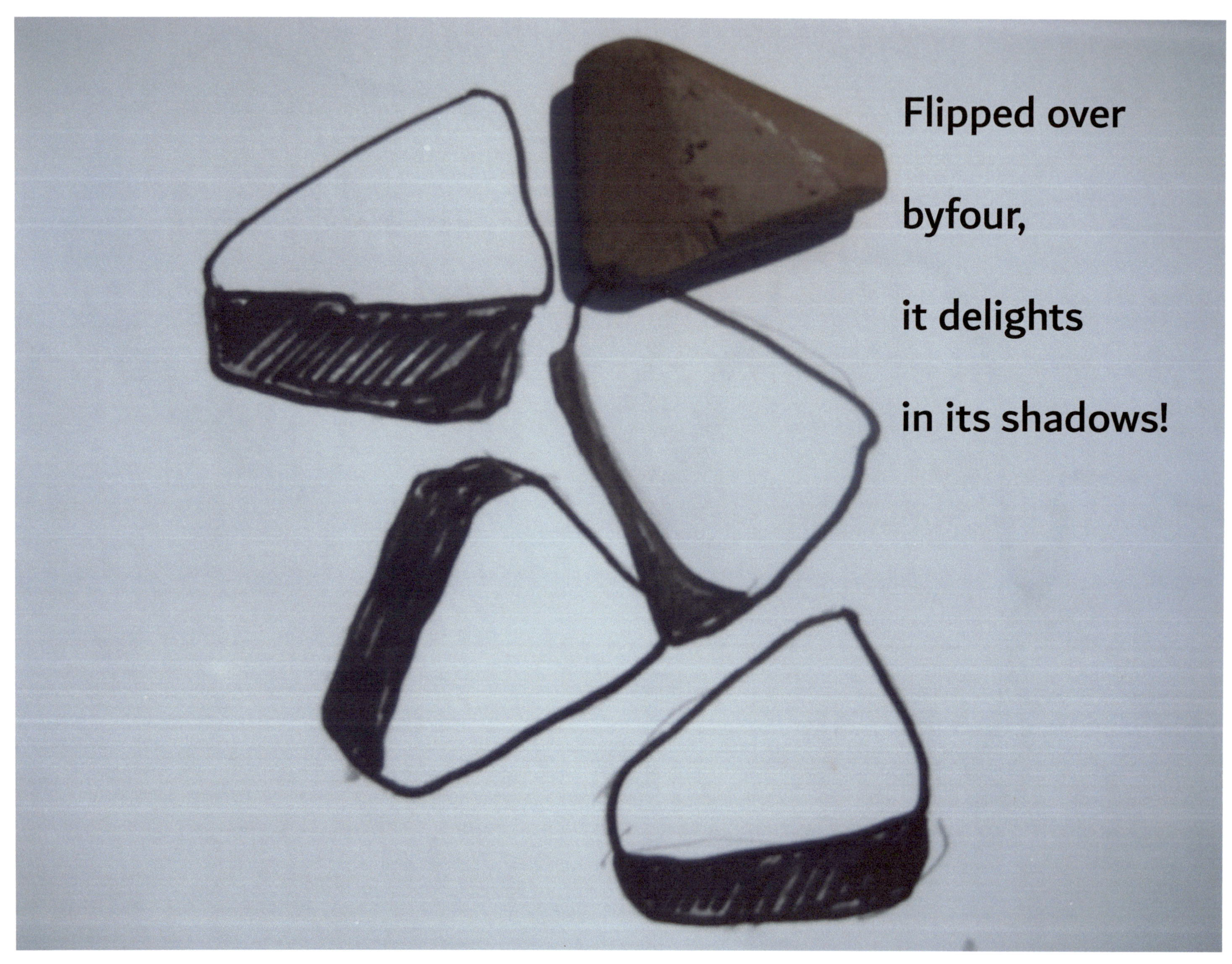

Flipped over
byfour,
it delights
in its shadows!

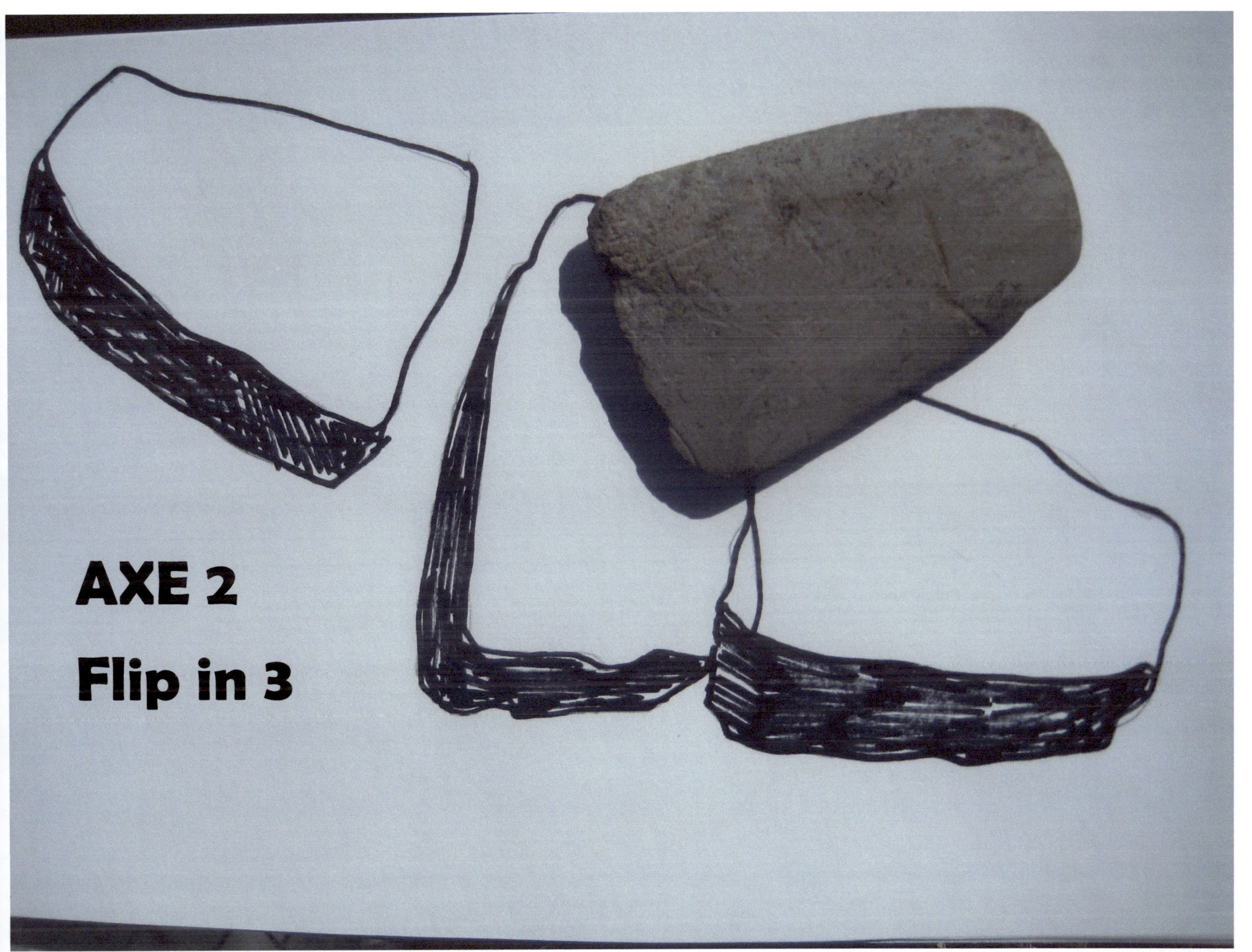
AXE 2
Flip in 3

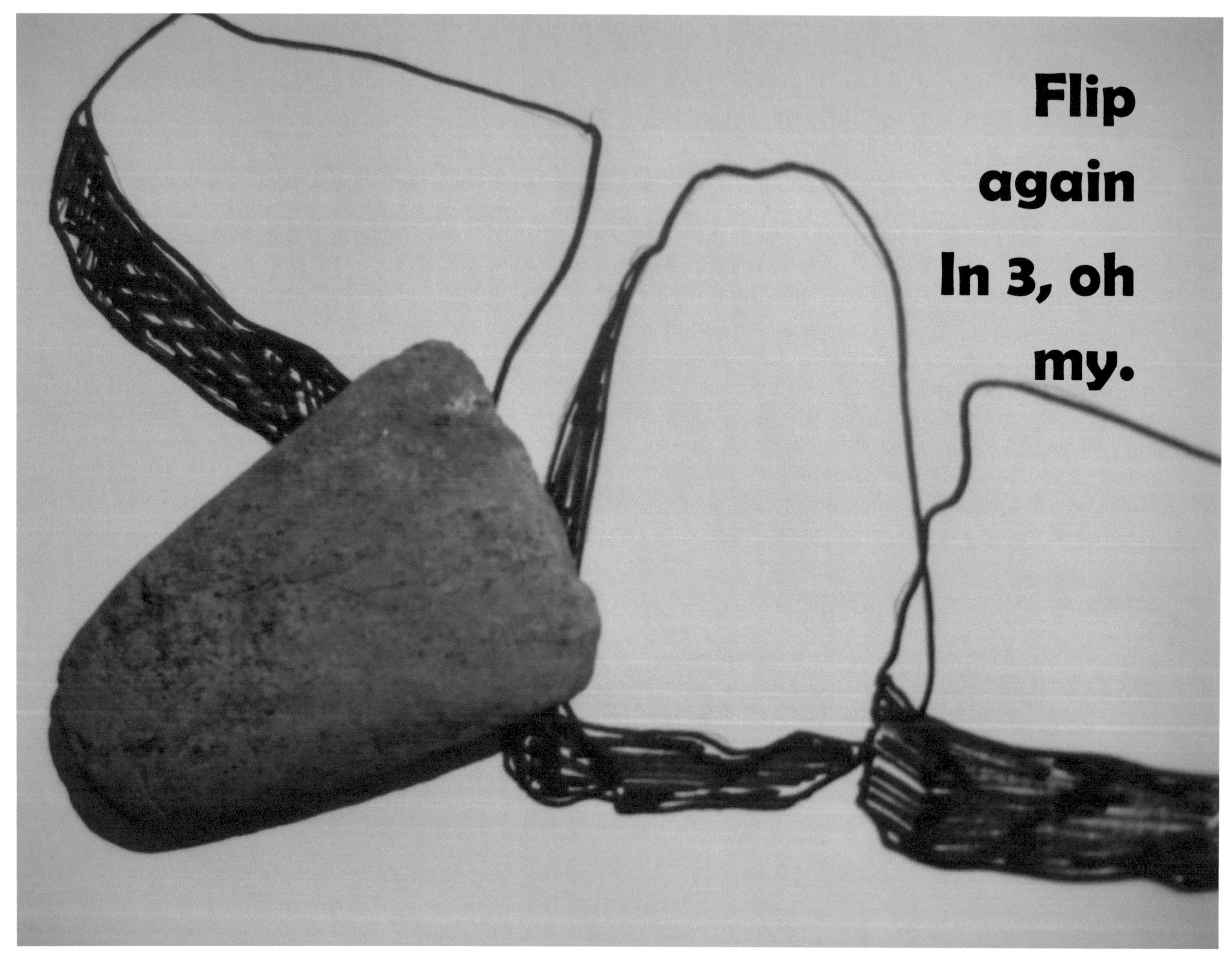

Flip
again
In 3, oh
my.

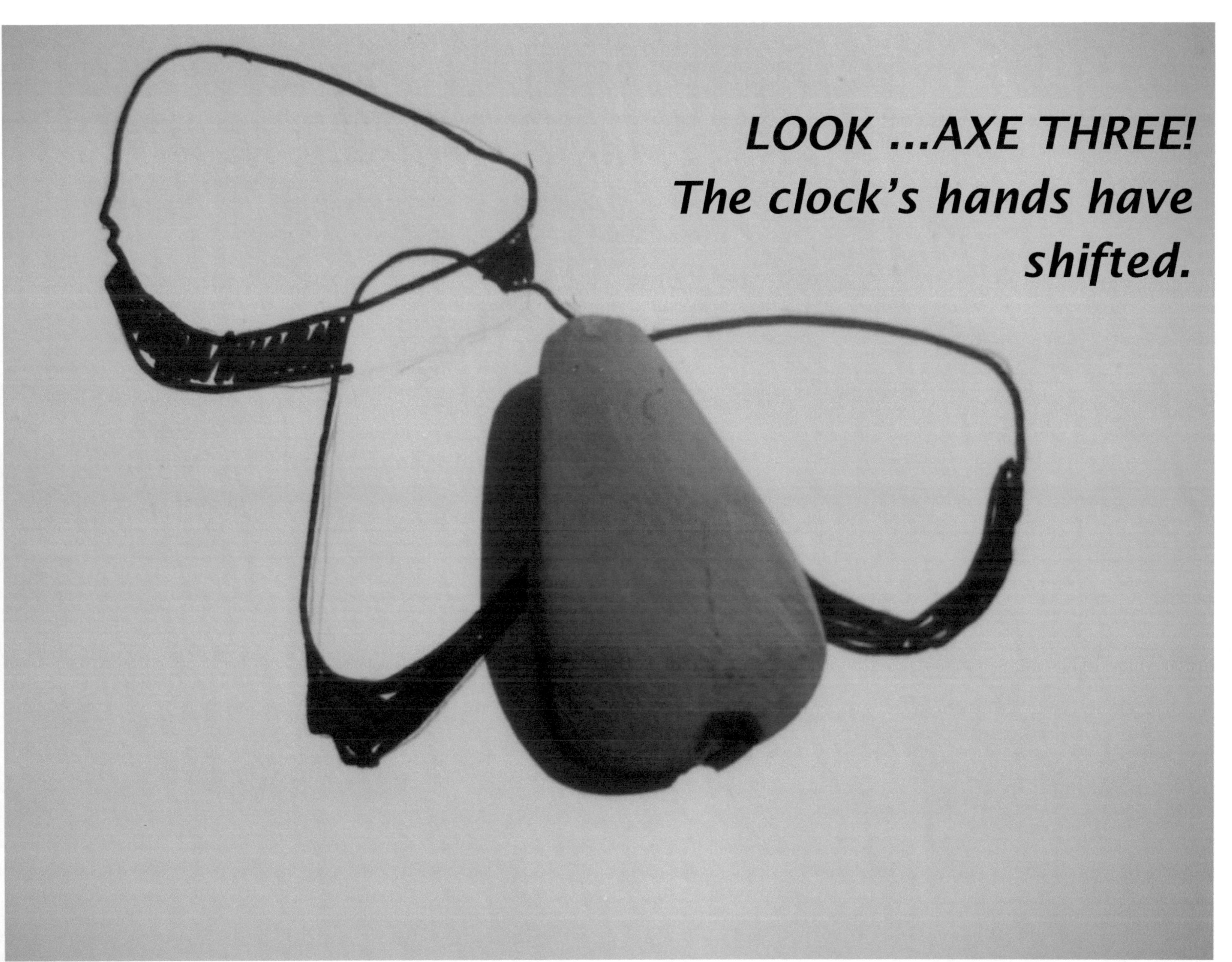

LOOK ...AXE THREE!
The clock's hands have shifted.

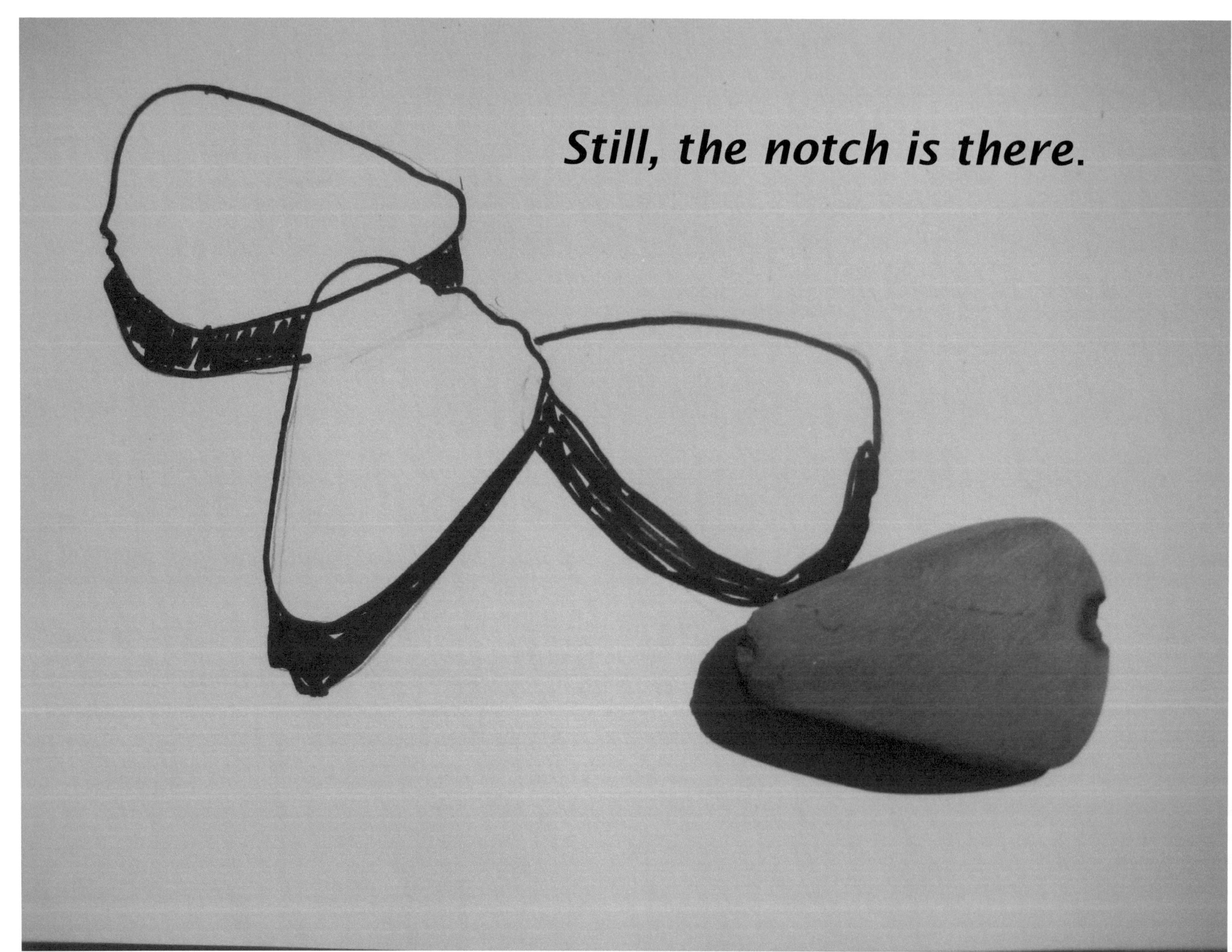Still, the notch is there.

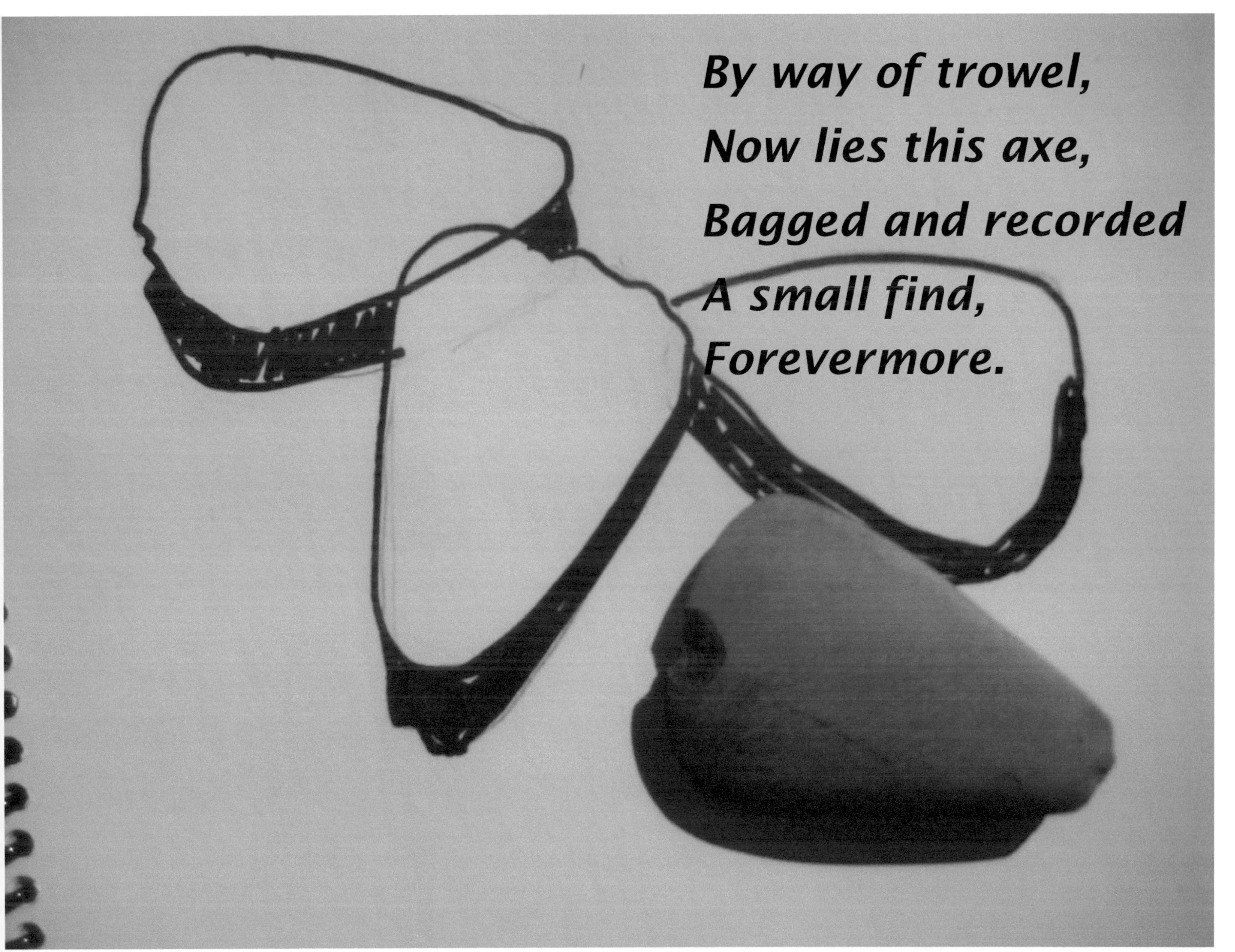

By way of trowel,
Now lies this axe,
Bagged and recorded
A small find,
Forevermore.

I have been volunteering with the Ness of Brodgar team since 2011 and through that and my connection with Antonia Thomas, I went to one of Scotland's smallest islands, Wyre.

As the Scottish Rangers at Orkney's World Heritage site say, "If you scratch the surface of Orkney, it bleeds archaeology."

I have continued to be involved in Orkney archaeology and in 2018, was invited to be one of the artists in residence. One of my favourite dog walks is around the Ring of Brodgar, which also inspires my artwork.
To see more of my art and to purchase: **https://JeanneBouzaRose.com**
https://JeanneBouzaRose.me
More about my 2018 Ness residency: **https://ArtWorksoftheEarth.com**

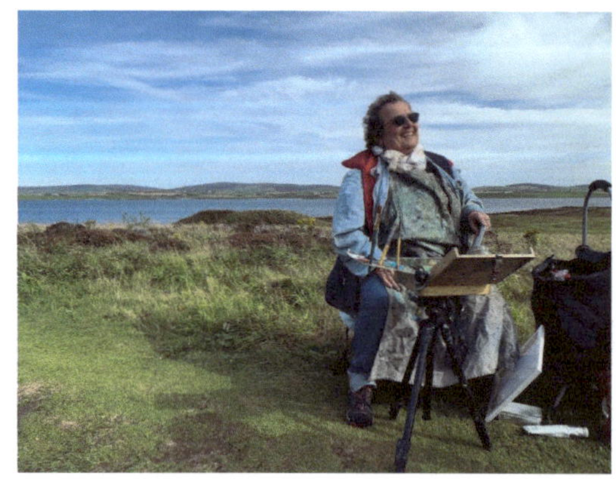
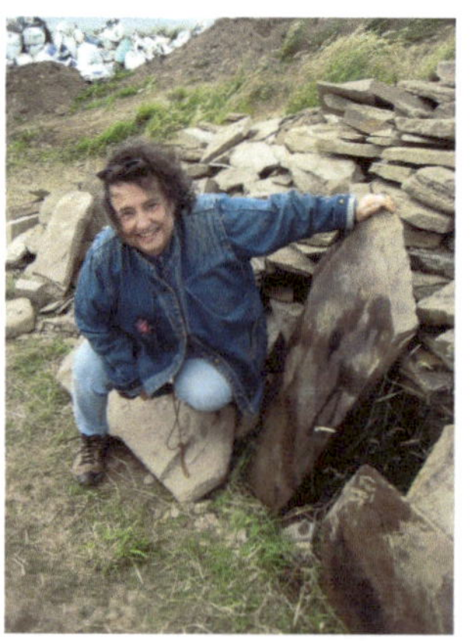

PHOTO above thanks to Leslie Joy. All other photos, Jeanne Bouza Rose